LOVING
ANGELS

This book belongs to

D1449807

Published by:
Modus Vivendi Publishing Inc.
3859, Laurentian Autoroute
Laval, Quebec
Canada H7L 3H7
or
2565 Broadway, Suite 161
New York, New York 10025

Graphic Design: Marc Alain
Translation: Brenda O'Brien
Photo Credits:
Cover 1: ©Vatican Museums & Galleries, Rome/SuperStock;
Cover 4: ©SuperStock
Page 1: ©Saint-Etienne Cathedral, Bourges, France/Lauros-
Giraudon, Paris/SuperStock; Page 2: ©Stock Montage/SuperStock;
Pages 3 and 5: ©Vatican Museums & Galleries, Rome/SuperStock;
Page 48: ©Pinacoteca di Brera, Milan, Italy/SuperStock

Legal Deposit: 2nd Quarter, 2000
National Library of Canada
Cataloguing in Publication Data
Therrien, Laurette
    Loving Angels
    (Heartfelt Series)
    Translation of: Sagesse des anges.
    ISBN 2-89523-020-X
    1. Angels. 2. Wisdom. 3. Angels - Pictorial works.
    I. Title. II. Series.
BL477.T4313 2000   291.2'15   C00-940560-7

Canadä We acknowledge the support of the Government of Canada through the
Book Publishing Industry Development Program for our publishing activities.

LOVING
ANGELS

Laurette Therrien

MV Publishing

"Angels are eternal, therefore they have no gender."
Auguste Comte (1798-1857)

When you think of it, angels are strange and asexual creatures, beings of pure light, sent to us directly from God, intended purely to protect us.

More often than not, cherubs are pictured as bodiless beings floating in the air, with beautiful curly hair and pink or golden wings covered with the softest of down. They seem to stare into the distance and smile incredulously at the folly of human beings.

In other instances, they take on the looks characteristic of an insolent and chubby Cupid, ready to shoot a magical arrow into any target all too human and all too weak to resist the torments of love.

Then again there are the majestical protective angels, armed with huge and widespread wings, the reflection of wisdom itself, whose very presence seems to assuage the pangs of human existence. These are the superior angels, the Archangels.

And then there are those closest to God, the Seraphim, the Cherubim and the Thrones, pure spirits, diaphanous and disembodied, unattainable by any ugliness found in the real world.

But regardless of what type of angel we choose to believe in, their presence is tangible at specific times, in magical moments, when the best possible conditions come together to transform us — mere humans that we are — into happy, carefree and optimistic beings inhabited by the spirit of that very special angel assigned to protect us.

"So many angels are in the air around us, we see it as transparent."
The Tragedians

The following is a poem I learned in elementary school and that I still remember today, many a decade later. Unfortunately, I've forgotten its author's name.

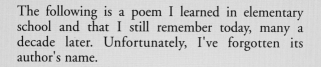

Dimples

A long, a very long time ago
A beautiful Angel saw a child
Sleeping, all white and pink
Under a rosebush heavy with blooms

The Angel approached softly
Fearful of waking the child
And with the tips of his fingers touched
Both corners of the sleeping child's mouth

The child was so beautiful
That the angel was enchanted
He wondered: could this be a brother of mine
Escaped or fallen to earth?

But the Angel, after touching the child,
Saw that he was wrong
And a bit sadly said to himself:
Alas!, as he flew back to the clouds

But on the child's two cheeks
The angel's fingers left two marks
And since this very happy event
Every child's smile is dotted with dimples

Did you know that...

... angels are considered to be purely spiritual creatures, intermediaries between God and human beings.

... theologians explain that sages have distinguished three *hierarchies* among angels, which are further subdivided into three *choirs*:
1. the *Seraphim*, the *Cherubim* and the *Thrones*;
2. the *Dominations*, the *Virtues* and the *Powers*;
3. the *Principalities*, the *Archangels* and the *Angels*.

... the *angelfish* is any of several brightly coloured, spiny-headed butterfly-fishes (*Holocanthus* and *Pomacanthus*) which have a compressed body and are found in tropical shore waters.

... *angelism* is the desire to achieve a state of extreme purity or otherworldliness.

... *angelica* is the name of umbelliferous plants cultivated in Europe for their aromatic odour and medicinal root and for their stalks, which are candied and eaten.

... an *angel's* bed is a bed having a suspended or bracketed canopy of less than full length.

... an *angel's footstool* is a term some people use to describe a skysail or a flying kite.

Be An Angel

Reach for the stars
Keep your halo polished
Share your favourite things with others
Plant a garden for the butterflies
Say something nice to someone every day
Be patient with those who don't fly as fast as you do
Talk to the plants to help them grow
Always tell the truth
Think good thoughts
Sprinkle a little star dust wherever you go.

Author Unknown

Angels

Angels are love, angels are light,
Angels are above, they have no fright,
Angels are beautiful in every way,
Angels want you to come and play,
Angels are delicate just like the rose's petal,
And angels' wings are as shiny as the brass kettle.

Adrienne Mullins

Acrostic

A question: to whom have you given your heart?

No doubt you have given it truly

Go on your way, knowing that I love you dearly

Even though life may try to separate us

Love of my life, we are together forever.

"Humans mask the worst in themselves with the most beautiful of angels that they can find."
Marguerite d'Angoulême (1492-1549)

Perhaps Marguerite d'Angoulême expressed a thought that we should all consider.

Our guardian angel, the angel that prevents us from making the worst of mistakes, that keeps us from giving in to our worst urges, may well be the very being of purity and justice that hides the more or less laudable intentions each of us would be well-advised to hide.

Instead of perching on our right shoulder, our guardian angel covers us like a blanket, like a shawl. Definitely an image to contemplate, to think about at length...

© Fontainebleau, Château/Lauros-Giraudon, Paris/SuperStock

Aunt Angelina's
Osso Bucco

1 veal shank, cut into bite-size pieces
30 g/1/4 cup flour
2 tablespoons olive oil
2 tablespoons butter
1 teaspoon salt
freshly ground pepper
2 chopped onions
1 teaspoon dried basil
1 can of Italian tomatoes
60 ml/3/4 cup white wine
1 cup beef consommé
2 teaspoons lemon peel
minced garlic
chopped parsley

1. Coat veal with flour.
2. Brown in oil and butter mixture.
3. Add salt, pepper, onions and basil.
4. Cover and simmer for approximately 15 minutes.
5. Add white wine and beef consommé.
6. Cover and simmer over low heat for approximately 2 hours, until the veal is well cooked.
7. Add the lemon peel, garlic and parsley shortly before serving.

Serve with salad and wholewheat pasta or with freshly-baked French bread.

"Unless a beautiful woman happens to be an angel,
her husband is the the unhappiest of men."

J.-J. Rousseau (1712-1778)

Acrostic

Certainly, love is charming

Harmony is one of its jewels

Even though we may doubt it

Rapture is something it holds

Usually very illusive

But all the better to hold

Sublime are its joys and exquisite its rewards.

"Man is neither angel nor animal and unfortunately, he who strives to be seen as an angel is often seen
as an animal."

Pascal

"In ancient times, donkeys who encountered angels
were said to be given the gift of speech. In our times,
some encounters give men the gift of braying."

Victor Hugo

© Arena Chapel, Cappella Degli Scrovegni, Padua, Italy/SuperStock

My Angel

We met in the month of May, the **month of angels** some people say. He appeared to me in all his magnificence, tall, haughty and a tad arrogant. Instinctively, I resolved to make him wait — all too often I'd had my joyous wings clipped. I had no intention of mistaking someone very ordinary for someone **angelic**. Soon I was caught up in my very own game, no **angel** I. We met everywhere: bars, cafés, parks, and we would walk for hours on end, often discussing **how many angels could fit on the head of a pin**. Whenever we were at a loss for words, he would say: What an **angel** you are!

He spoke softly, all the better to charm me! And I found him positively enchanting when he willingly poured out his emotions: "You're my **guardian angel**," he would murmur. Goodness knows he was ever so flattering!

I know, I know, he tended to exaggerate. But oh! how charmingly and how convincingly! My heart took wing just hearing him!

He was an **angel in disguise** and when we first kissed, I melted. He would call me **Angel**, and sighing, I could but drop my wings and give in to his charms.

That night, in his arms, I was transported to Heaven and at the stroke of dawn, he awoke me with a kiss, tenderly whispering: "Your smile is the smile of an **angel**." All I could answer was: "No **angel** was ever so happy, in heaven or on earth!"

L.T.

Did you know...

... that according to Emanuel Swedenborg, a British scientist and philosopher (1688-1772), angels are souls who have chosen Heaven; that if one of them simply thinks of another angel, that angel instantly appears and that angels can communicate with one another.

... that Swedenborg also believed that the world of Angels is governed by Love and that regardless of where they happen to look, they always see the face of God. Although a man of science, Swedenborg also claims that the clothing of Angels shines and reflects their respective degree of intelligence.

... that the name *Los Angeles* means "The Angels" and more than 3 million people live in the Southern California city — not all of them angels!

Give! So that God, who provides for all families
May give your sons strength,
and your daughters grace
So that your vines bend with ripened fruit
So that your barn be filled with golden wheat
So that you may be a better person;
so that you may see the Angels
As they travel through your nighttime dreams!

Victor Hugo (Excerpt, *For the Poor*)

Taking Flight
Episode 1

I didn't know I was an angel
Until I grew wings.
You think I'm dreaming? Perhaps.
But how can we be sure that dreams are not reality
And vice versa.

Granted, they are very, very small
My wings
And very, very white
With a touch of pink where they touch my skin

I am a very young angel, you see
A cherub, in fact
I am so young, I am unable to fly
At least not yet

I seek a kind soul
Willing to teach me
To take me under their wing
Can you understand what I mean?

**"Pure angels, radiant angels,
Carry my soul to the heavens!"**

M. Carré and J. Barbier
for Gounod's opera, *Faust*

Raphael's Angel-Food Cake

1 cup egg whites
1 pinch of salt
120 g/1 cup cake flour
300 g/1 ^{1}/2 cup granulated sugar
1 teaspoon cream of tartar
1 teaspoon vanilla essence or lemon juice

- Add salt to egg whites and mix.
- Add the cream of tartar and beat until firm.
- Mix in sugar gradually.
- Mix in the sifted flour, 30 g/^{1}/4 cup at a time.
- Add the vanilla essence or lemon juice, stirring gently.
- Pour into a large, ungreased bundt cake pan.
- Place in an unheated oven and set at 150°C/ 300°F.
- Bake for approximately 50 minutes.
- Remove from oven; place mold on a rack.
- Let cool for approximately 1^1/2 to 2 hours; remove cake from mold.
- Decorate with whipped cream and berries.

If you eat a piece of this delicious cake and it doesn't make you feel as if you've grown wings, I promise to lay down my apron and enter the world of spirits forevermore.

Taking Flight
Episode 2

As I was saying, not everyone who has wings
Can fly. But no one would listen.

Of course, I saw no one on the horizon
Angels refuse to fly so low
So I waited, I passed the time
I called out, I whistled

I wanted to dance
But you have no idea
How heavy they are to carry
Outspread wings
They don't weight a feather
They are as heavy as an anvil

Oh, well! I sighed
Someone is sure to come along
A good Samaritangel
Generous, in no particular hurry
With plenty of experience
Willing to initiate me

Full flight, gliding flight
Night flight, Fancy flight
I want to try them all
I want to reach the sky

"Man yields to the angels and accepts
death solely through the infirmity of his pitiable
will."

Edgar Allan Poe (1809-1849)

Taking Flight
Episode 3

I was wrong all along the line
The glorious angel taking flight
Resplendent in white and pink
Is, in fact, a myth
So much more work is required

You know, the idea of a guardian angel
I was sure was one invented by you
Human beings that you are
To gain some reassurance
To feel less alone
To feel as if someone was watching over you

Oh, how wrong I was
Guardian angels do exist, indeed
I am the living and saddened proof
My wings weren't given me to fly
With my best effort I can only flap them
Strongly enough to perch on the shoulder
Of my guardian angel, who does exist
Please forgive my ignorance
Please forgive my disarray

"The place occupied by angels is filled only slowly
— rare are the elderly who die enjoying the grace of
God."

Father de Saint-Cyran (1581-1643)

Taking Flight
Episode 4

What would you have me think?
Some people even claim
That I would not exist
Were it not for my shadowy alter ego
Perhaps they are right
But still, I am my opposite's reflection
I am his mirror image
We two are equally beautiful

No? You think me vain?
I am, in my own way, a guardian angel
A being of light
A protective wing
And still, you would want me humble!

It is I whom you have spoken to
Since a day lost in the mists of time
It is I you seek for advice and protection
I, the guardian of your existence
Ever vigilant, ever watchful

I am proud, perhaps
But rightfully so
Be indulgent with me
Recognize my valour
Be grateful!

Taking Flight
Episode 5

Yes, I know, I know
The story began with my wings
Surely I was given them for a reason
Otherwise why bother?
Otherwise who could explain?

To summarize the story
I used to be a cherub
But now I have grown
And believe me, I'm no fool
In fact, God made me quite intelligent
And I think I understand

Angels have no one to count on
They have to live life as it comes
All alone, on their own
I have had no mother
Nor will I have any special friends
My life will be a very special one!

But wait, wait!
I hear a soft voice
It is a human voice
My companion is you
I am perched on your shoulder
Let me lean on you
As you lean on me

Amen

♐

"The Earth is to the Sun what Man is to Angels."
Victor Hugo

"I will not wish thee riches, nor the glow of greatness,
But that wherever thou go some weary heart
Shall gladden at thy smile,
Or shadowed life know sunshine for a while.
And so thy path shall be a track of light,
Like angels' footsteps passing through the night."

> (Words on a church wall
> in Upwaltham, England)

"But if these angel beings guard you, they do so because they have been summoned by your prayers."

> Saint Ambrose

"Every man hath a good and a bad angel attending on him in particular, all his life long."

> Robert Burton. 1576-1640

"Hush, my dear, lie still and slumber!
Holy angels guard thy bed!
Heavenly blessings without number
Gently falling on thy head."

> A Cradle Hymn
> Isaac Watts. 1674-1748

"I want to be an angel,
And with the angels stand
A crown upon my forehead,
A harp within my hand."

Urania Locke Bailey

"To the most lovely, the most dear,
The Angel, and the deathless grail
Who fill my heart with radiance clear -
In immortality all hail."

Charles Baudelaire

"It is not because angels are holier than men or
devils that makes them
angels, but because they do not expect holiness
from one another, but from God alone."

William Blake

"My delight and thy delight
Walking, like two angels white,
In the gardens of the night."

Robert Bridges

"The reason angels can fly is because they take
themselves lightly."

G. K. Chesterton

"To love for the sake of being loved is human, but
to love for the sake of loving is angelic."

Alphonse De Lamartine

"The angels are so enamored of the language that is
spoken in heaven that they will not distort their lips
with the hissing and unmusical dialects of men, but
speak their own, whether there be any who understand it or not."

Ralph Waldo Emerson

The Angelica Plant

Angelica, also called *archangel*, is an umbelliferous plant of the genus Angelica. It is found mainly in the Northern Hemisphere, where it grows in humid locations, and mostly in mountainous areas.

It is a wild plant whose decorative foliage can grow to over four feet tall. However, it can also be grown in gardens. Its stalk is hollow and its leaves have from five to seven bright green folioles. Its flowers are concave and parasol-shaped.

Better known in Europe, its stalks (in the summertime) and its roots and seeds (in the autumn) are widely used. Its characteristic odour makes it very easy to recognize.

Angelica has stimulating, stomachic, expectorant and sudorific properties. It is used as a herbal tea to stimulate the appetite and to counter digestive problems and anemia.

It also has carminative properties, in other words it helps relieve flatulence. It is also used to relieve respiratory problems (asthma, chronic bronchitis, smoker's cough, colds), colic and rheumatism.

Used as a mouthwash, angelica is very effective to prevent bad breath.

Multipurpose Angelica

- In pastries, its stalks are candied and used to flavour and decorate cakes, quick breads, soufflés, etc.
- When cooked with angelica, acidic fruits taste sweeter.
- When macerated in brandy, it produces ratafia liqueur.
- Served with fish, it is an excellent condiment.
- It can be used to flavour vinegar.
- Its essential oil or its macerated stalks can be used to produce various alcoholic beverages such as Chartreuse, gin and ratafia.

Angelica Tea

Roots: Add 1 tablespoon of roots to one cup of water and boil for 5 minutes.

Seeds: Add 1 tablespoon of seeds (or leaves) to one cup of water and boil for 5 minutes; let steep for 10 minutes.
Drink lukewarm.

Symbol

In the mysterious language of plants and flowers, angelica symbolizes *inspiration* and *ecstacy.*

"The man, who has seen the rising moon break out of the clouds at midnight, has been present like an archangel at the creation of light and of the world."

Ralph Waldo Emerson

"Make friends with the angels, who though invisible are always with you. Often invoke them, constantly praise them, and make good use of their help and assistance in all your temporal and spiritual affairs."

Saint Francis de Sales

"If I have freedom in my love,
And in my soul am free,
Angels alone that soar above,
Enjoy such liberty."

Richard Lovelace

"The guardian angels of life fly so high as to be beyond our sight, but
they are always looking down upon us."

Jean-Paul Richter

"It is not known precisely where angels dwell —
whether in the air, the
void, or the planets. It has not been God's pleasure that we should be
informed of their abode."

Voltaire

"Outside the open window
The morning air is all awash with angels."

Richard Purdy Wilbur

"Make friends
With the Angels,
Who though
Invisible are
Always with you..."

Saint Francis De Sales (1567-1622)
French Bishop

"Angels may deliver
A message
From the realms of glory.
Or they may work, unsung,
Unseen, in ways we can only
Begin to think about."

Timothy Jones
20th-century writer

"Angels are the first
and most excellent creation."

B. Herder Houck
20th-century English cleric

hen you think of it, angels are strange and asexual creatures, bein
pure light, sent to us directly from God, intended purely to protect
re often than not, cherubs are pictured as bodiless beings floatin
air, with beautiful curly hair and pink or golden wings covered with
test of down. They seem to stare into the distance and smile incred
sly at the folly of human beings. In other instances, they take on
ks characteristic of an insolent and chubby Cupid, ready to shoo
gical arrow into any target all too human and all too weak to resist

man beings. In other instances, they take on the looks characteristic
insolent and chubby Cupid, ready to shoot a magical arrow into a
get all too human and all too weak to resist the torments of love. Th
ain there are the majestical protective angels, armed with huge a
espread wings, the reflection of wisdom itself, whose very presen
ms to assuage the pangs of human existence. These are the super
gels, the Archangels. And then there are those closest to God,